CW00859165

I AM OF IRELAND

By SEAMUS FINNEGAN

© WILD GOAT PRESS 2018

Printed by Wild Goat Press 2018

Copyright © 2018 Seamus Finnegan

ISBN-13: 978-1987665482

Cover design by Ken McClymont

For the Living and the Dead.

ACKNOWLEDGEMENTS

Thanks to Faber & Faber, 74-77 Great Russell Street, London WC1B3DA for permission to quote from The Poetry of Derek Walcott 1948-2013 and from NORTH by Seamus Heaney.

Thanks to Wild Goat Press and Blake Everitt.

Thanks to Ken McClymont, Penny Gold, Carolyn Cummings Osmond, Alexandra Allen-Smith, and Kimmi Dewey.

SEAMUS FINNEGAN has written over 30 stage plays. They have been produced in London, Israel and the USA. Seven volumes of his work have been published – NORTH, THE CEMETERY OF EUROPE, both by MARION BOYARS LTD; JAMES JOYCE AND THE ISRAELITES. IT'S ALL BLARNEY, and DEAD FACES LAUGH, all by HARWOOD ACADEMIC; AFTER PARIS and TWO JEWISH PLAYS by WILD GOAT PRESS – available on Amazon.

I AM OF IRELAND will be published simultaneously with MicMac production at OLD RED LION THEATRE in June 2018. Past productions of Finnegan's work at OLD RED LION include SOLDIERS, directed by Julia Pascal in 1981; DEAD FACES LAUGH, LIFE AFTER LIFE, DIASPORA JIGS, MURDER IN BRIDGPORT, WAITING FOR THE ANGELS and SPINOZA; all directed by KEN McCLYMONT

Other details about SEAMUS FINNEGAN can be found on his Wikipedia page, Writers Guild website and on SEAMUS FINNEGAN at Amazon.

KEN MCCLYMONT: Scottish theatre director and artist. He has directed plays by living playwrights including: John Byrne, Iain Heggie, Chris Lee, Howard Brenton, Greg Freeman, Caryl Churchill, David Edgar and Seamus Finnegan. Former artistic director of the Old Red Lion Theatre, AFTER PARIS is his eighth collaboration with Finnegan. His paintings have been exhibited in London, Brussels, Glasgow, Edinburgh, various galleries in the south of France and are in private collections in the UK, USA and CANADA. For further information, see www.kenmcclymont.co.uk.

I AM OF IRELAND is scheduled to be first performed at the OLD RED LION THEATRE, LONDON on Tuesday 5th June 2018.

The play will be directed by KEN McCLYMONT.

Cast at time of going to press: SHENAGH GOVAN, EUAN MCNAUGHTON, SARIA STEEL, RICHARD FISH, SEAN STEWART, JEROME NGONADI, ANGUS CASTLE-DOUGHTY.

N.B. Some minor changes may be made to script during the rehearsal period.

DRAMATIS PERSONAE

THERESA MAHON
JOSEPH MAHON
MARY MAHON/SISTER MARIA
DOMINIC
BISHOP FOLEY
FATHER ADAMS
MRS FITPATRICK
JACINTA REID
BARRY SHORT
FATHER FLANNAGAN
DETECTIVE MAGEE
SGT O'HARE
NURSE BURNS
HARRY
SEAN
PETER
DEREK
BELFAST DETECTIVE
SAMMY NELSON

Other parts played by cast. The play can be performed by 6/7 actors with appropriate doubling/trebling of parts.

PROLOGUE

ENTER THE ENTIRE CAST.

DRESSED AS FOLLOWS:

1. NIGHT CLUB DRAG QUEEN IN HIGH HEELS, SUSPENDERS ETC. WEARING GREEN SASH THAT READS 'MOTHER IRELAND'.

2. 'TERRORIST' IN COMBAT JACKET, BLACK BERET, DARK GLASSES AND CARRYING A HURLEY STICK.

3. BISHOP IN MITRE AND ROBES.

4. ORANGE MAN IN BOWLER HAT, SUIT,

   ORANGE SASH.

5. RUGBY PLAYER IN GREEN JERSEY, WHITE

   SHORTS AND CARRYING RUGBY BALL.

6. NUN, IN FULL HABIT

THEY SING ANTHEM—'IRELAND'S CALL'.

INDIVIDUAL LINES/VERSES/CHORUS TO BE WORKED OUT

IN REHEARSAL.

1

'COME THE DAY AND COME THE HOUR

COME THE POWER AND THE GLORY

WE HAVE COME TO ANSWER

OUR COUNTRY'S CALL

FROM THE FOUR PROVINCES OF IRELAND

CHORUS:

IRELAND, IRELAND

TOGETHER STANDING TALL

SHOULDER TO SHOULDER

WE'LL ANSWER IRELAND'S CALL

2

FROM THE MIGHTY GLENS OF ANTRIM

FROM THE RUGGED HILLS OF GALWAY

FROM THE WALLS OF LIMERICK

AND DUBLIN BAY

FROM THE FOUR PROVINCES OF IRELAND

CHORUS

3

HEARTS OF STEEL

AND HEADS UNBOWING

VOWING NEVER TO BE BROKEN

WE WILL FIGHT, UNTIL

WE CAN FIGHT NO MORE

FOR THE FOUR PROVINCES OF IRELAND

CHORUS

EXIT /LIGHT CHANGE.

SCENE 1

GALWAY. HOME OF THE MAHON FAMILY.

THERESA AND JOSEPH, AND THEIR DAUGHTER,

MARY.

THERESA	Have you heard what she said?
JOSEPH	I heard.
THERESA	She 'thinks' she has a 'vocation'. She wants to be a nun.
JOSEPH	I heard what she said.
THERESA	And having heard, what do you have to say about it?
JOSEPH	It's not for me to say anything much. It is a decision for Mary herself.
THERESA	Jesus wept! Is that all you're going to say. It's our daughter we're talking about here.
JOSEPH	I know who my daughter is.
THERESA	I'm not sure I do. A nun? A nun? No young woman in her right mind these days 'wants' to be a nun.
JOSEPH	Our daughter does.
THERESA	It's not the past when maybe it was the only way for a woman to get an education and a position….
JOSEPH	You think all those vocations in the past were just

	about getting a position?
THERESA	No. But now? Today? There are so many opportunities for women. Why would you want to waste yourself....your life....by entering a convent.
MARY	Mother!
THERESA	Don't you mother me. You're going to break my heart, Mary Mahon. That's what you're doing with your 'vocation'. After all I....we....have done for you. I don't understand. I don't understand it at all.
	THERESA RUSHES OUT, WEEPING.
	SILENCE.
MARY	I didn't think she'd take it so hard.
JOSEPH	She'll come round.
MARY	Will she?
	PAUSE.
JOSEPH	It's not as if it's something you announced completely out of the blue.
MARY	I 'have' talked about it.
JOSEPH	And maybe she thought or wanted to believe, it was just that. Talk.
MARY	You know I am serious....don't you?
JOSEPH	I do, And maybe I've seen it coming for a long

	time.
MARY	You have?
JOSEPH	Fathers can have intuition too you know, Mary Mahon.
	MARY SMILES. PAUSE.
MARY	Should I go to her?
JOSEPH	No. Let her be for a while. She needs to weep and rage alone for a bit. I'll talk to her later.
MARY	I think I'll go for a walk….if that's alright….
JOSEPH	Of course. You need to think alone as well.
	PAUSE.
	MARY GOES TO LEAVE.
JOSEPH	Mary?
MARY	Yes, Dad?
JOSEPH	You're sure?
MARY	I'm sure.
	HOLD/LIGHT CHANGE.

SCENE 2

SOUND OF LAMBEG DRUM.

ENTER, AS IF IN SLOW MOTION FORMATION AND IN SILENCE, A GROUP OF MASKED PEOPLE/WHOLE CAST, DRAPED IN UNION JACKS AND/OR ULSTER FLAGS. A MAN CARRYING LAMBEG DRUM BEATS OUT A SINISTER RHYTHM. ANOTHER, WELL-SUITED AND BOOTED, IN BOWLER HAT AND ORANGE SASH, MARCHES IN STEP TO DRUM. THEY MOVE DOWNSTAGE TO FACE THE AUDIENCE.

SILENCE.

LIGHT ON EDWARD CARSON.

CARSON	Protestant People of Ulster……
ALL	Protestant People of Ulster…..
CARSON	Recite after me….
ALL	Recite after me….
CARSON	Ulster Will Fight……
ALL	Ulster Will Fight…..
CARSON	Ulster Will be Right…..
ALL	Ulster Will be Right…..
CARSON	Always. Always.
ALL	Always. Always.

CARSON	We will fly the flag of the British Crown…..
ALL	We will fly the flag of the British Crown……
CARSON	We will give our blood for the British Crown….
ALL	We will give our blood for the British Crown……
CARSON	Ulster Will Fight…..
ALL	Ulster Will Fight….
CARSON	Ulster will be Right….
ALL	Ulster will be Right………
CARSON	Protestant People of Ulster…..
ALL	Protestant People of Ulster…….
	VOICE OF ONE OF THE MARCHERS.
VOICE	Look! There's one.
ALL	Look! There's one.
VOICE	A fuckin Paki…….
ALL	A fuckin Paki…..
VOICE	Kill the bastard!
ALL	Kill the bastard!
VOICE	Kill…..
ALL	Kill. Kill, Kill,
	THE CHANT BUILDS TO A CRESCENDO.
	SOUND OF LAMBEG DRUM GETS LOUDER AND
	FASTER. LOUDER AND FASTER.
	EXIT.

SCENE 3

SILENCE.

ENTER DOMINIC, WEARING BALACLAVA.

HE REMOVES BALACLAVA. TURNS TO LOOK OUT

AT AUDIENCE.

DOMINIC   This is where they made me a Catholic. A Roman

Catholic! Saint Patrick's Roman Catholic Church in

Donegall Street, Belfast. Northern Ireland. Built in

1874 with the help of money raised by the

Protestant community. As was the first Roman

Catholic Church in Belfast. Saint Mary's in Chapel

Lane. Not many people know that. If they do, it's

not remembered. History contains a lot of what is

forgotten. Or deliberately Ignored. But this…..this

is where it happened. The Baptism!

The Christening! The renouncing of the devil on

my behalf by my godparents. An uncle, once an

actor, now dead. An aunt, also dead, emigrated

to America, like manys another Paddy in search

of………..

It was here, by this baptismal fount, one morning

in March four years after the Second World War

had ended, that I, Dominic Magee, had the Holy

14

Water poured over my head and the priestly words pronounced - I baptise Thee in the Name of the Father and of the Son and of the Holy Ghost. Amen. I knew nothing of it. I was asleep. 'You didn't stir or cry like most babies do', my mother told me years later. I didn't know if this was a matter of pride for my mother or a hint of chastisement since she claimed that I slept through most things in life ever after. The rest was to follow….the preparation at school for the First Confession and the First Holy Communion.

A young, white-haired priest, a Father Kelly, immaculate in black suit and clerical collar examined us on our knowledge of the Catechism. Who is God? God is our Father in Heaven, the Creator and Lord of all things. Why do we call God our Father? We call God our Father because He gave us Life and provides for us with fatherly care.

Has God a beginning? God had no beginning. He always was and always will Be; He is Eternal. What is Confirmation? Confirmation is the sacrament through which the Holy Ghost is given to us, with His graces and His seven gifts, to make us strong and perfect Christians and soldiers of Jesus Christ.

Why does the Bishop give those he confirms a stroke on the cheek? The Bishop gives those he confirms a stroke on the cheek to remind them that they are soldiers of Christ and that for His sake they must be ready to suffer anything, even death itself, rather than deny the faith.

I remember that stroke on the cheek by the Bishop. I can feel it. I remember too the words that seemed to sear themselves onto my soul – Soldiers of Christ. Suffer. Death. Faith.

DOMINIC SINGS A VERSE OF 'FAITH OF OUR FATHERS'. BREAKS OFF.

Divis Street. Falls Road. Belfast. Northern Ireland.

This is where I made myself into an Irish Republican. A group of us fourteen, fifteen year old school boys in the black blazered, black and yellow tied uniform of Saint Mary's Irish Christian Brothers Grammar School, Barrack, dandered up one lunch time to gawp at the window of the then Republican headquarters. The window that the fevered Reverend Ian

Paisley and his cohorts had smashed in order to remove the Tricolour flag that had been draped forlornly and defiantly on display. This was the era when Republican flags and emblems were illegal. Banned from view and the psyche, even in a Catholic ghetto. Riots had followed this symbolic desecration by the Free Presbyterian preacher man….he, who seemed unaware that his Presbyterian forefathers had hoisted the Republican flag over the city of Belfast in celebration at the Fall of the Bastille. Presbyterians in those days were members of the United Irishmen. Rebels against the English Crown.

Ah the ironies of history. There were stones and bricks and broken bottles strewn around from the night before's clash with the RUC and B Specials. A class mate from the Lower Falls had participated in the riots and been arrested. Another class mate, son of a fruit and vegetable merchant and who lived in a big house near Fruithill Park, had an argument with one of the Christian Brothers, about what he claimed was the irrelevance of Irish flags and emblems when all the coins in our pockets had the Queen's head upon them.

Economics. Not symbols. That's what mattered, said the boy from the Big House who had more halfcrowns in his pocket than anyone else in the schoolyard. Some of whom had never seen a half crown. The boy was arrogant. Knowing. And very brave. And as things turned out, he was probably a bit of a prophet. But my sympathy was with the boy who had been arrested. I looked at him from afar when he returned to school a day or so later. He was smiling. Energised. Not cocky. Not heroic. Not bragging. Just knowing. Knowing in a different way from the half crown merchant. Names and dates began to circulate. Patrick Pearse. James Connolly. 1916. Wolfe Tone. 1798. Clusters of short-trousered Catholic Grammar schoolboys whispered, argued, shouted and yelled. New friendships. New alliances. New enemies were formed and unformed. The war with my own Antrim Roaded Castle Catholic mother began. These political shenanigans were NOT what my passing the 11 plus and going to the Irish Christian Brothers Grammar were supposed to achieve for the son of Mary Burns! Even if his grandfather on HIS father's side, had been a Pearse volunteer and fought in 1916 and the Civil War. The more my mother poured scorn on the green, white and orange, the more her son immersed himself in the quagmire of its history. And worse was to come for Mary Burns. The devout early Mass going little boy who had once prayed for a vocation to the priesthood, STOPPED going to Mass. Refused to take the Sacraments. Bunked off school to go and sit in the Belfast Central Library. And read plays and books written by that atheistic socialist 'protestant' George Bernard Shaw AND stare at the legs of the shortskirted protestant girls from the Methodist College.

Oh the times they were a-changing.

DOMINIC SINGS THE BOB DYLAN SONG.

LIGHT CHANGE/EXIT.

SCENE 4

ENTER BISHOP FOLEY AND FATHER ADAMS.

BISHOP   What can I offer you, Father Adams?

FR ADAMS   What are you thinking of, Your Worship?

BISHOP   I am having a small Jameson. Will you join me?

FR ADAMS   A small one. Thank you.

BISHOP   A small Jameson before lunch helps the digestion
            I think.

            THE BISHOP POURS A SMALL WHISKEY WHICH HE
            HANDS TO FR ADAMS AND A SIMILARLY SMALL
            ONE FOR HIMSELF BUT THEN ADDS THE SAME
            AGAIN.

BISHOP   Sit down, Father Adams. Sit down.

            FR ADAMS SITS. BISHOP SITS OPPOSITE HIM IN
            LARGE ARMCHAIR.

            And how is life down in the country?

FR ADAMS   Quiet.

BISHOP   It is? I always found the country very noisy. Did
            you know I was a curate in a country parish one
            time?

FR ADAMS   I didn't know that.

BISHOP   It was a long time ago. Not long after I was
            ordained. I tell you, Father Adams, if anything

	challenged my vocation, it was the three years I spent as a country priest. The smells you get in the country. All that manure and what's this they call it….silage! Saints preserve us but that stuff gives off a devilish pong.
FR ADAMS	The countryside does have its challenges, Your Worship.
BISHOP	Give me a city any day of the week. I was born in a city. I like walking in a city. I like the buildings, the pavements, the people strolling and bustling about. There's life in a city. And sin….which keeps us in business, Fr Adams.
FR ADAMS	Yes. Indeed.
BISHOP	In the country parish I spent three trying years. I felt the people were just waiting….waiting ….to die. It was nearly the death of me.
FR ADAMS	People die in cities.
BISHOP	They die everywhere, Father Adams. But in cities, things happen before death arrives. The Pope is a city boy. I think it shows. I've never been to Buenos Aires but I imagine it is a grand city full of sinners sinning. What do you make of our new Pope. Francis?
FR ADAMS	I……….

BISHOP	Here, let me get you another small one. It'll lubricate the thoughts.
	BISHOP POURS DRINKS. AS HE DOES SO, HE STUDIES FR. ADAMS WHO AVERTS THE BISHOP'S GAZE. HOLD. LIGHT CHANGE.

SCENE 5

DUBLIN. ST STEPHEN'S GREEN.

FR FLANNAGAN, A PRIEST FROM THE CARIBBEAN, SITS ON A BENCH.

HE IS READING A BOOK ABOUT LIBERATION THEOLOGY. HE IS NOT WEARING CLERICAL CLOTHING.

ENTER BARRY, A YOUNG MAN IN EARLY TWENTIES.

HE SEES 'THE BLACK MAN'. STOPS. THEN WALKS OFF/EXITS.

SILENCE.

RE-ENTER BARRY. WALKS SLOWLY BEHIND THE BENCH. STOPS. STARES AT 'THE BLACK MAN'. FR FLANNAGAN TURNS ROUND TO LOOK AT BARRY.

SILENCE.

FR FLANNAGAN	Can I help you?

BARRY RUNS OFF/EXITS.

FR FLANNAGAN WATCHES HIM GO. SHRUGS.

RETURNS TO READING HIS

BOOK.

SILENCE.

SUDDENLY, BARRY RUNS ONTO STAGE, WEILDING

A KNIFE. HE RUNS TOWARDS FR FLANNAGAN AND

STICKS KNIFE INTO 'THE BLACK MAN'S' STOMACH.

THEN RUNS OFF.

FR FLANNAGAN CLUTCHES HIS STOMACH.

LIGHT CHANGE.

SCENE 6

A CEMETERY.

ENTER HARRY AND SEAN, TWO MEN IN THEIR

LATE SIXTIES.

HARRY	What made you come back for his funeral?
SEAN	He was an important friend when we were all young men.......remember?
HARRY	Who told you he was dead?
SEAN	I have my contacts.
HARRY	You do?

SEAN	The convent in these parts is the centre of communications.
HARRY	Eh?
SEAN	My cousin is a nun. She saw it in the newspaper and told me.
HARRY	It must be a long time since you'd seen him.
SEAN	It is. Nearly thirty years...maybe more.
HARRY	And you'd had no contact with him all those years?
SEAN	No. I heard....read the odd thing about what he was doing.
HARRY	He never mentioned you. Except one time he came back after he and Enya had been over to London.
SEAN	That would've been the last time I saw him.
HARRY	Said something about you drinking expensive bottles of wine and frequenting fancy restaurants.
SEAN	We went to Ronnie Scott's Jazz Club. We all got quite drunk.
HARRY	He said.
SEAN	I wrote to him after his father died but I never heard back from him.
HARRY	So, are you over for long? Or is this just a flying visit for the funeral?

SEAN	I fly back tomorrow morning.
HARRY	Do you come over much?
SEAN	Occasionally….to visit the cemeteries. Most of those I knew are dead. The mother and father and…….
HARRY	There's a lot of dead people in here.
SEAN	I thought Jimmy Madden might have been at the funeral.
HARRY	I haven't seen him.
SEAN	Do you ever see him?
HARRY	Used to bump into him in town……….but not in ages. Has marriage problems I gather. Are you married? I noticed the ring.
SEAN	I am.
HARRY	Somebody told me you were divorced.
SEAN	I was.
	SILENCE.
SEAN	And Mike is dead.
HARRY	He's been dead years….years….Wasn't thirty when he died. Brain tumour.
SEAN	No news of Kevin?
HARRY	No. He went to England as well. Liverpool, wasn't it?
SEAN	I noticed in town, the café's gone.

HARRY	What café?
SEAN	Peter's Café. OUR café. The one we spent many hours in...days, months, years.
HARRY	That's been gone ages....ages. But then if you weren't here, you wouldn't know.
SEAN	It was our headquarters. And himself (INDICATES THE GRAVE) was the President.........the chief of staff.........
	FREEZE
	CROSSFADE TO PETER, A BELFAST BORN ITALIAN. HE WEARS A WHITE CATERING JACKET.
PETER	They used to come in here everyday after school. Sometimes during school for they were infamous for what they called 'going on the hike'. There were six of them, all told. The big fella with the tweed jacket. It was obvious he was the leader of sorts. An Irish language enthusiast. I used to rile him by saying, 'And what good is learning Irish going to do for you. There's no jobs in Belfast where speaking Irish is a requirement'. He used to throw back his head and smile. 'You'll see. Someday you'll see', he replied. I was right. I'm nearly always right. There are no jobs where it's a requirement. But fair play to him. He made his

own job. He and his eventual wife were involved in setting up one of those Irish schools. The ones where the kids learn everything through the medium of Irish. I'm not sure what sort of a job they get afterwards. But it was a movement that grew during the course of the' troubles'. And I understand the school's still going. Got the Government funding and everything. It was sad to hear of his death. Sixty eight years of age he was. Died at the end of last year. Big funeral I gather. In St Mary's, Chapel Lane. The Mass was in Irish. Another one of them....the one with the long hair...it was the fashion then with the Beatles and the Rolling Stones.....he left. Went to England. To live in sin in London. He used to call in sometimes when he was home. Bit of a rebel he was. Liked to think he was any road. He used to sit in here waiting, waiting for the girls from Methodist College to arrive. He had an eye for the girls. Protestant girls. I used to say to him, 'If you paid as much attention to your studies as you do to those wee hussies, you might get somewhere'. 'Don't worry, he'd say, 'I'm on my way round to the Central Library soon. To eye up more women'.

I'd answer, 'Damned the study you're doing'. Though I did hear he ended up lecturing at a University somewhere in England. God alone knows on what subject. Probably 'Women's Studies'. The little fella with the moustache and the bad skin died young. Brain tumour, they said. Collapsed in the avenue of an Antrim Road hotel after a poker and drinking session. That was the end of him. Didn't make it to thirty. The other fella of small stature, with the big smile, married an English girl. Lived in Liverpool. Had a nervous breakdown. Nothing heard of him since. The one whose father once owned a pub in York Street where the RUC and Special Branch men drank after hours, he stayed in Belfast. Married. Had children. Continued working in various bars in the city. He called in on a regular basis. I always felt a bit sorry for him. He was a gentle, intelligent fellow. Maybe the brightest of them all. Had a scientific mind. He had wanted to study medicine but the bar work and marriage...it's an old story isn't it? And finally, there was the one who got himself arrested during a riot before 'the troubles' proper had started. It was that time the Reverend

Paisley removed the flag from the Republican headquarters just up the road a bit from here. 1963? 1964? He'd left school earlier than the others. Labouring on building sites. But sometimes he'd join them in here in his working clothes and cement boots. Came under the influence of the tweed jacket fellow, learnt Irish and did teacher training….eventually. What did they all talk about when they were in here in my café? Religion. The five proofs of Aquinas. Politics. The long haired one was always banging on about George Bernard Shaw and socialism. Literature. The tweedy Gaelic enthusiast had a passion for P. G. Woodehouse which puzzled me not a little. And of course there was talk about girls. Women! They muffled their voices then. But I heard them. And I remember what they said about whether Protestant girls were 'freer' than Catholic ones. I soon put a stop to that kind of talk and they'd return to debating Aquinas and the five proofs. And there you have it. Six young men from Belfast. Catholics of the 1960's. All of them educated by the Irish Christian Brothers and what became of and not became of them. But there'll be more. Oh yes, a lot more…..to tell…..

LIGHT CHANGE.

SCENE 7

GALWAY. THE MAHON HOME.

THERESA AND JOSEPH.

JOSEPH	Weren't you educated by nuns, Theresa?
THERESA	I was. At primary school and Grammar.
JOSEPH	And am I right in saying that over the years I have heard you speak of them in glowing terms?
THERESA	You are. There was the odd old bitch but generally speaking….
JOSEPH	And am I right in saying that I have listened to you over the years say that three quarters of Ireland wouldn't be able to read or write if it wasn't for them. The nuns and the Christian Brothers.
THERESA	You are.
JOSEPH	And am I also right in saying that I have heard you rage against the Media, the TV and the politicians, who, you have said, are only too keen to talk about the sexual scandals of recent years and not the enormous contribution the nuns and brothers

and priests made to the education and lives of the very people who are now in the media, television and politics.

THERESA   Hypocritical bastards!

JOSEPH   That was the phrase you used.

THERESA   So?

JOSEPH   So? So why are you so against what our daughter, Mary, has decided for herself?

THERESA   It's hardly the best time to be joining the Church in Ireland is it?

In Periculo Mortis.

JOSEPH   Pardon?

THERESA   It means 'in danger of death', Joseph. And that's where the Catholic Church is in Ireland today. Disgraced priests, bishops, brothers and nuns. And those who aren't in disgrace are in despair. Despair at the behaviour of their disgraced colleagues. Despair that they are lumped in together with those disgraced. Despair that the people have lost all respect for them. Despair that the faith that once unified the country is lost. Have you, Joseph, ever heard or listened to how young people talk about the clergy? To them, they are all perverts, paedophiles, sexual deviants.

JOSEPH	I have heard such comments….yes….
THERESA	And our daughter….our beautiful, bright, intelligent daughter is wanting join that decaying, dying institution……
	SILENCE.
JOSEPH	It is a brave thing to be doing.
THERESA	Brave? Brave? It's stupid, Joseph. And you know it.
JOSEPH	You said she was bright. Intelligent.
THERESA	Not on this, she isn't.
	SILENCE.
JOSEPH	Maybe, Theresa, 'we' have become infected.
THERESA	What are you talking about, Joseph? Infected! Us….
JOSEPH	Maybe we ourselves have become sick…..
THERESA	I'm not sick. You speak for yourself.
JOSEPH	Maybe…we….I….and you….have lost the ability to understand……
THEERESA	Understand what?
JOSEPH	'Faith'.
THERESA	Faith and understanding don't sit together, Joseph.
JOSEPH	Precisely, Theresa. Precisely. But our daughter, Mary Mahon, seems to me, to have 'faith'. She

has what we have lost......what Ireland has lost.......

HOLD/LIGHT CHANGE.

SCENE 8

A POLICE STATION IN BELFAST.

DEREK AND A POLICE DETECTIVE.

DET   Name?

DEREK   Who's asking?

             Derek. Derek Smith.

DET   Age?

DEREK   Fifty four.....Eighteen.

DET   Address?

DEREK   121 Kings Park, Newtownabbey, ULSTER. The

             World.

DET   Occupation?

DEREK   Spaceman.

             Unemployed. All the Fenians and foreigners get

             the jobs. But it's going to change. Big Brexit Arlene

             has Mrs May by the balls.

DET   Where were you last night, Derek?

DEREK   At home. Watching porn. Ever watch porn,

             Detective. Never?

DET	Why are you lying, Derek?
DEREK	I'm not lying. I was at home. Ask my Da.
DET	We did.
DEREK	Fucker!
DET	We have CCTV footage, Derek.
DEREK	Bully for you. Porn's better.
DET	Of you and others at a rally.
DEREK	No law against that. Or aren't loyalists allowed to meet these days on our own streets?
DET	You were shouting slogans.
DEREK	Not allowed to speak these days either….
DET	You were also seen throwing stones and petrol bombs at a house.
DEREK	Are you a Taig, Detective? Loads of Taigs in the police these days.
DET	The house belonged to a Mister Muhammad Assad.
DEREK	Pakis everywhere these days. Taigs. Pakis. Poles. Niggers.
DET	Who do you like, Derek?
DEREK	White Ulster Protestants. We are the people. Ulster is Right. Ulster will Fight.
	DEREK STARTS SINGING – GOD SAVE OUR QUEEN.
	ENTER A POLICE CONSTABLE. HE WHISPERS TO

DETECTIVE.

EXIT POLICE CONSTABLE.

DET	You have a good singing voice, Derek.
DEREK	Maybe I'll be a rock star, Detective.
DET	Maybe.

DETECTIVE GOES TO LEAVE. TURNS.

DET   Something you should know, Derek. Mister

Muhammad Assad?

He's dead!

LIGHT CHANGE

SCENE 9

ENTER DOMINIC.

DOMINIC   This......this is where my Trade Unionist bricklayer

father set the foundations for making me into a

socialist. Casement Park. Andersonstown Road.

Belfast. Northern Ireland. Home of the Gaelic

games in Ulster. The GAA. Gaelic Athletic

Association. Or the G Ha Ha as my mother

mockingly referred to it. Casement Park. Named

after Roger Casement. Executed for treason by

the English Government. Treason as defined by

the English....anyone who opposes English rule

and supremacy. I played Gaelic football in
Casement. A rare sporting heroic day against
Armagh CBS. I scored two goals and two points.
Played a blinder that day If I say so myself. Made
more poignant and symbolic in that our school
team jerseys were the same yellow as the County
team. Antrim County. My county. The county of
my birth. Jesus, I was a proud wee fucker that day.
But on another day. The day of the 50th
anniversary pageant to commemorate 1916. The
Easter Rising. The Rebellion. My father walked me
round to Casement Park to sit on the concrete
terrace and watch the colourful pageant. Tricolours
and Starry Ploughs wafting in the breeze. Celtic
designed costumes of Irish dancers jigging,
hornpiping and reeling. Gaelic footballers and
hurlers and camogie players uniformed in Persil
white shorts cutting great swathes through the
emerald green pitch in choreographed patterns
from corner flags to centre spot. Fiddlers. Flute and
whistle players, accordionists, bodhran drummers
working up cacophonic medleys of Irish airs. And a
platform….a raised scaffolded stage facing the
Stand side upon which stood Seven Men. Seven

Days. Signatories of the Proclamation of the Irish Republic as read from the steps of the GPO in Dublin by Patrick Pearse. But Pearse was not why my father had brought me here….for he digged me in the ribs as he said – 'Here's our man now….the workers man ' – as the public address system announced the name of….JAMES CONNOLLY! Revolutionary socialist. Founder of the Irish Citizen Army who was also to be executed in the yard of Mountjoy Prison strapped to a chair, too wounded to stand to face the English firing squad. My father's earthly creed was Socialism. My father, who was thrown out of the confessional box by a priest in Brompton Oratory, London, during the war when he foolishly and comically dared to suggest that after hearing a speech at Speakers Corner in Hyde Park, he was thinking….maybe….maybe of joining the Communist Party. And in his innocence the advice of the oratoried English priest as to how this might square with being a cradle Catholic? It was on that day in Casement Park that the utopian dream was passed from father to son. DOMINIC SINGS 'THE INTERNATIONALE'.

LIGHT CHANGE.

DOMINIC   I was seventeen years of age when I first stood

here. Sixth form. The Irish Christian Brothers had

brought us up here on a three day retreat to St

Clements Redemptorist monastery. We were

young men about to embark upon life's journey.

And the Brothers thinking was to give us a

spiritual preparation for that journey. I can smell

the bread. White slices of a big pan loaf. The

odour from the refectory seemed to permeate the

whole Retreat House. The food was good. Big

plates of steaming stew. And Father Finlay. He

was the priest in charge. The director of the

retreat. Fierce big man with a booming voice. And

hands. Father Finlay had the hands of a

heavyweight boxer. He put the fear in us, I can tell

you. It was the second night of our retreat. We'd

had the Confessions earlier in the afternoon. I

remember fellas bragging about what they had

said to the priest in confession. How they had

made up sins of impurity that they only wished

they had committed. To see what reaction they'd

get from the priest and how much penance they'd

be given. Mostly, it was just one Our Father, three

Hail Marys and a Glory Be. There was the odd one or two got a decade of the rosary and one fella got all five decades. The Sorrowful Mysteries! We muttered this information to each other as we walked about the grounds after the evening meal. The vow of silence we were supposed to observe got broken I'm afraid.. And then the bell rang to summon us to the chapel for the night prayers and sermon. Father Finlay mounted the pulpit like a Redemptorist colossus. You could hear the silence. Nobody seemed to be breathing. He that power did Father Finlay. He blessed himself-In the Name of the Father and of the Son and of the Holy Ghost. Amen. He started the sermon. Jesus, what a sermon that man preached. I do not remember exactly what he said but I remember the effect to this day. He made the sermon in Portrait of the Artist seem like a light hearted Sunday school chat. He said he was aware that some of us that afternoon had probably not made a good confession. He knew that there were wags among us who had probably made a sacrilege of the sacrament of penance and had added a mortal sin to the sins already blackening our souls. And if that was the case, we better make quick reparation in front of the Tabernacle now and plead for God's forgiveness. If we didn't and died in the night, hell is what faced us. And we would burn. Burn! Burn! Imagine those occasions he said when your finger accidentally touches the end of your cigarette. It burns. It hurts. And in a reflex action we quickly remove our finger. But in Hell, he said, there will be no reflex reactions. Just the burning for eternity multiplied a billion times more painful than that cigarette burn. And not just our fingers but our whole bodies. BURNING. BURNING. For ETERNITY. ETERNITY! Something the length of which we cannot possibly fathom because there is no end to eternity. After the sermon we were allowed to take the air, smoke a cigarette and look out over Belfast Lough at the shipyard cranes and the city lights down to our right and the lighthouse lamp to our left where the boats sailed out up the lough into the open sea. There was no sound to be heard that night from the boys of the Irish Christian Brothers Grammar School. Only the crackling of the gravel under our feet. The wags and wiseguys of earlier silenced. All of us pacing to and fro alone with our consciences and fearing the moment when the bell rang to tell us to retire to our study bedrooms for the night. Everyone of us knowing, seeing in our minds eye the crucifix that hung above our single beds. The crucified Jesus, who every time we committed a sin, was crucified all over again. Every one of us….knowing….believing….terrified in the knowledge that this night could be our last. We may not waken to see the sun shimmer on the waves of Belfast Lough or play watery shadow games with shipyard cranes. We may never return to the city that lay below us. We may never again see our mothers and fathers. That night, at St Clements Retreat House, hard men from the Falls Road and elsewhere quaked in their souls. And yet….and yet…..soon it was to be all so different……..

LIGHT CHANGE/MUSIC---BEATLES-REVOLUTION.

EXIT.

SCENE 10

ENTER BISHOP AND FATHER ADAMS.

BISHOP He's certainly cut from a different cloth than the

last one.

FR ADAMS Who?

BISHOP The Pope. Francis.

FR ADAMS It seems to be the case, Your Worship.

BISHOP It was brave of him to step down, mind you.

FR ADAMS Or was he pushed?

BISHOP You're not suggesting that there were

shenanigans in the Vatican, Father Adams?

FR ADAMS No. No. I have no such knowledge.

BISHOP I know we are a universal Church and a Catholic is

a Catholic. But WHERE a man comes from has an

effect on the way he looks at the world. And a

German can't help himself but look at it through

German eyes. Luther was a German, Father

Adams.

FR ADAMS He was.

BISHOP Shall I let you into a secret as to what some of the

Bishops and Cardinals called Ratzinger? Ratsy!

Ratsy! (HE CHUCKLES TO HIMSELF)

FATHER ADAMS REMAINS STONY FACED.

	But Francis is an ARGENTINIAN! That'll be a different way of looking at the world altogether. Have you ever been to South America, Father Adams?
FR ADAMS	No I haven't.
BISHOP	One day, maybe. One day.
	PAUSE.
	It's got to be the heat. It makes a man warmer. More open. Poor old Ratsy was from a cold climate.
FR ADAMS	Like us, Your Worship.
BISHOP	True. True. But sure we have the uisce baite to warm us. Will we have another?
FR ADAMS	No. No. Thank you. Not before lunch.
BISHOP	After lunch I have things to do. Now's your chance. Are you sure?
BISHOP	Will I? Or wont I?
	BISHOP STANDS HOLDING WHISKEY BOTTLE.
	Maybe not. I don't want to be smelling too much of the drink and going into the lunch that Mrs Fitzpatrick has prepared. Have you met Mrs Fitzpatrick?
FR ADAMS	A woman showed me in when I arrived. If that was Mrs Fitzpatrick….

BISHOP	That was her. A grand woman is Mrs Fitzpatrick. An understanding woman. And one hell of a cook. What Mrs Fitzpatrick can do with potatoes, even soapy ones, is something that not even the angels in heaven know about.
	ENTER MRS FITZPATRICK.
MRS F	Lunch is more than ready, Your Worship.
	SHE GLANCES AT WHISKEY GLASSES AND SHAKES HER HEAD.
BISHOP	Have you met Father Adams, Mrs Fitzpatrick?
MRS F	Didn't I let him in when he arrived.
BISHOP	Of course. Of course.........when he arrived. I was just telling Father Adams what you can do with potatoes.
MRS F	Throwing them out is what I'll be doing with them if you don't hurry on and eat them. There's nothing worse than a cowl spud!
BISHOP	After you, Father Adams. Lead the way, Mrs Fitzpatrick.
	BISHOP WINKS AT FR ADAMS.
	Aren't women a wonder, Father Adams? Where would we be without them?
MRS F	Not here. That much I know. Not any of you.
BISHOP	Ah, Mrs Fitzpatrick, you're such a theologian at

	times.
MRS F	So why don't you listen to us more?
BISHOP	Mrs Fitzpatrick thinks there should be women priests. And we should all be allowed to marry.
MRS F	Tiocfad ar lar. Our day will come!
	ALL EXIT / LIGHT CHANGE.

SCENE 11

	DUBLIN. POLICE/GARDA STATION.
	ENTER DETECTIVE MAGEE AND OFFICER O'HARE.
MAGEE	What the feck is going on in this country? The victim's a priest for Christ's sake.
O'HARE	Would it matter if he wasn't?
MAGEE	A knife attack is a knife attack.
O'HARE	In broad daylight. In St Stephen's Green.
MAGEE	Do we know the name of the victim yet?
O'HARE	We do. His name is Father Patrick Flannagan.
MAGEE	Jesus!
O'HARE	He is from Montserrat in the Caribbean. Over here at some kind of Theological conference before he takes up a position in a parish in County Clare.

MAGEE	Short of priests in County Clare, are they?
O'HARE	Short everywhere it would seem.
MAGEE	He's part of a 'Black Mission', is that it?
O'HARE	Could be, Detective. Could be.
MAGEE	What news of the attacker?
O'HARE	We have arrested a young man seen running down Grafton Street. His name is Barry Short. Twenty three years of age. Originally from Cork.
MAGEE	Feckin Cork! I hate Cork.
O'HARE	Why's that, Detective? It's a nice city, Cork. It's not Dublin. But then nowhere is.
MAGEE	I knew a woman from Cork….once…..
O'HARE	They do have them in Cork. Women.
MAGEE	It was a long time ago. Never mind that. Don't why it came into my head.
O'HARE	Pain can linger, Detective. My mother told me that. Wise woman, my mother. Told me all sorts of things.
MAGEE	You talk a lot about your mother, O'Hare.
O'HARE	I'm Irish
MAGEE	What news of the knife used?
O'HARE	Found in the bushes in St Stephen's Green. Near the bust of James Joyce.
MAGEE	Jesus. It would be him.

O'HARE	Who?
MAGEE	Never mind. Never mind, O'Hare. Is he ready for interview, this Barry Short?
O'HARE	He's ready alright.
MAGEE	Do you think it was he who stabbed the black Father Flannagan?
O'HARE	Shall we try to find out?
MAGEE	After you, O'Hare.
O'HARE	Thank you, sir.
	EXIT/CROSSFADE TO HOSPITAL WARD.
	FATHER FLANNAGAN IS SITTING UP IN BED,
	READING THE SAME BOOK AS BEFORE.
	ENTER NURSE BURNS.
NURSE BURNS	Are you comfortable, Father? How are you feeling? Lucky, it wasn't deeper, eh?
FR FLANNAGAN	I am comfortable. I am feeling better. And yes, lucky. Thank God.
NURSE BURNS	Terrible the things going on these days in this country. And in broad daylight. And you sitting in the Green, reading your book. This country is going to the dogs altogether. There's too many foreigners. That's what's doing it.
FR FLANNAGAN	I am a foreigner.
NURSE BURNS	Oh yeh, I suppose you are. But you're a priest.

	That's different.
FR FLANNAGAN	How so?
NURSE BURNS	It just is. You know what I mean.
FR FLANNAGAN	Do I?
NURSE BURNS	I would leave. Emigrate, if I could
FR FLANNAGAN	Where to?
NURSE BURNS	Anywhere. Anywhere, to get the hell out of this place. I hate Dublin. But it's probably too late for the likes of me.
FR FLANNAGAN	Where are you from, Nurse Burns?
NURSE BURNS	Belfast. I hate it as well. That's why I left and came here. To Dublin.
FR FLANNAGAN	Why do you hate your native city?
NURSE BURNS	All that sectarian stuff. Does my head in. Catholic. Protestant. I can't be bothered with it anymore. They say there's the Peace Process but I was up in Belfast around the last Twelfth. 12th of July. That's when the Orangemen march. And I'll tell you, Father, there's still a lot of hate around. The way yon fellas were banging those Lambeg drums....frenzied like. You knew. You just knew that every bang on the drum was a Catholic head being smashed. Dublin's bad. But Belfast?
FR FLANNAGAN	There seems to be a lot of hate in Ireland.

NURSE BURNS	Not just Ireland, Father. It's everywhere. Have you ever watched the TV News recently? But what about you? How come YOU are in Dublin?
FR FLANNAGAN	I am....I was attending a Theological Conference.
NURSE BURNS	Do you like Dublin? You probably don't after what's happened to you.
FR FLANNAGAN	I like Dublin. It is a very fine city. Irish people are friendly and warm hearted.
NURSE BURNS	Like the fella that stuck a knife in you?
FR FLANNAGAN	Maybe even he, Nurse Burns.
NURSE BURNS	Do you think he was on drugs? There's a lot of those young 'uns off their heads with all sorts of substances. How long are you here for?
FR FLANNAGAN	Well, I don't know. After the Conference, I was to take up a post in a Parish in County Clare.
NURSE BURNS	County Clare! Saints preserve us!
FR FLANNAGAN	You hate County Clare as well?
NURSE BURNS	No. No. I've never been. But it seems a strange place to be sending a 'foreign' priest.
FR FLANNAGAN	There is a shortage of priests in County Clare. In Ireland.
NURSE BURNS	That's because of the sex scandals. People have lost faith in the clergy. In the Church.
FR FLANNAGAN	Have you?

NURSE BURNS	I don't bother with all that much these days. I probably shouldn't be telling you this but I don't go to Mass these days. I still go at Christmas. I like to see the crib and hear the carols. But it's years since I went to Confession. I've probably committed so many sins I've forgotten the half of them.

ENTER MATRON/SISTER.

MATRON	Have you forgotten you work in this hospital, Nurse Burns? There are other patients to be seen to.

NURSE BURNS SMILES AT FR FLANNAGAN WHO SMILES BACK.

EXIT NURSE BURNS FOLLOWED BY MATRON.

LIGHT CHANGE.

SCENE 12

A CEMETERY, HARRY AND SEAN, AS BEFORE.

HARRY   So, has England been good to you? Did you make the right decision leaving us?

SEAN   Who knows, Harry? Who knows?

HARRY   You must like it. You've been away for what….40 odd years?

SEAN   It's been a long time. Nearly twice as long as I lived here.

HARRY   Living amongst the enemy.

SEAN   The enemy still rules here. Even after 30 years of war.

HARRY   You weren't here for that.

SEAN   No. I wasn't.

HARRY   So, what is it about London made you stay?

SEAN   I like its cosmopolitan nature. It is the most cosmopolitan city in the world.

HARRY   I thought that was New York.

SEAN   London is more multi-ethnic than New York.

HARRY   Is it?

SEAN   I don't like places that are homogenous. Where I live in London has all sorts from everywhere in the world.

HARRY	We have our immigrants here.
SEAN	So I gather. And how is it?
	SILENCE.
HARRY	You're still teaching I hear at some University.
SEAN	I am.
HARRY	What is it your teaching?
SEAN	English Literature.
HARRY	Yer man (INDICATES GRAVE) taught Gaelic Literature.
SEAN	I know.
HARRY	So did I. Until I got sick. Had to stop. I haven't worked now for nearly 20 years.
SEAN	What was wrong?
HARRY	It's too long a story to tell now. You were never too keen on 'the Irish' were you? You never learned it like the rest of us. You never went to the Donegal Gaeltacht?
SEAN	No. I didn't.
HARRY	And you left.
SEAN	Yes. I left.
HARRY	She who left with you came home again. Married Matthew. He's one of the Gaeligoiri. They were at the Requiem Mass in the Church.
SEAN	I didn't see them.

HARRY	Which one of us I wonder will be next to join him in the Belfast/Milltown clay?
	THEY BOTH STARE AT THE GRAVE. HOLD.
	LIGHT CHANGE/MUSIC/GAELIC LAMENT.

SCENE 13

	CONVENT.
	MARY MAHON AND MOTHER SUPERIOR.
MOTHER SUPERIOR	Something's bothering you, Mary. What is it? You having doubts?
MARY	You told me once, Mother Patricia, that there is always doubt.
M.SUPERIOR	I said that?
MARY	You did. But no....it's not that....
M.SUPERIOR	What is it, Mary?
MARY	My mother's not taking too kindly to the idea of my becoming a nun.
M.SUPERIOR	Why's that, do you think?
MARY	I'm not sure.
M.SUPERIOR	Does she see it as 'losing' her daughter?
MARY	That might be part of it.
M.SUPERIOR	What might the other part be?

MARY	She is very agitated about what has happened to the Church in Ireland in recent times.
M.SUPERIOR	Understandable. It hasn't been an easy time in recent years, as we all know only too well.
MARY	But I don't think that's the real reason. My mother has never been one for 'thinking' what most think. She's always been a very independent thinker.
M.SUPERIOR	So what do you think is really bothering her about your decision?
MARY	Faith.....
M.SUPERIOR	Faith?
MARY	I think it's challenging her own idea of faith. I think it's causing her to ask questions about what she believes and doesn't believe. I think I have set off some kind of mental torment in herself.
M.SUPERIOR	Does your mother practise?
MARY	Does she go to Mass on a Sunday? Is that what you mean?
	MOTHER SUPERIOR SHRUGS/NODS.
MARY	Not regularly. Not every Sunday. My father does. He quite often goes off on his own to Mass on a Sunday morning.
M.SUPERIOR	But your mother doesn't go with him?

MARY	Now and again. But…..
M.SUPERIOR	Have you ever asked your mother why she doesn't go with your father?
MARY	No. Never.
M.SUPERIOR	Why not?
MARY	Didn't seem appropriate.
M.SUPERIOR	How do you think your father feels about your decision? Really feels?
MARY	I don't know. I'm his only daughter. His only child. He's always been supportive of all that I do.
M.SUPERIOR	Everything?
MARY	Maybe not everything.
	MARY SMILES.
M.SUPERIOR	Do you think your father has 'faith'? Or is going to Mass on Sunday just something he does. The habit of a cradle Catholic?
MARY	I don't 'know'. But I think my father has a very profound religious faith. He's a good, kind man.
M.SUPERIOR	There are good kind people who don't have religious faith, Mary. And some who do who are monsters….as we have witnessed in recent times. Mostly men. But we won't go there.
	MARY SMILES. SHE HAS HEARD THIS BEFORE FROM MOTHER PATRICIA.

M.SUPERIOR	But where does all this sit with you, Mary? Your mother and father are not contemplating entering religious orders. You are.
MARY	Yes. I am.
	SILENCE
M.SUPERIOR	Shall we go to the chapel and sit in front of the Crucifix on the altar for a while? You can light a candle. I always find lighting a candle can clear one's thinking…..temporarily, at least…..
	HOLD. MOTHER PATRICIA EXITS FOLLOWED BY MARY.

SCENE 14

	DEREK AND SAMMY NELSON IN JAIL.
DEREK	Are you really Sammy Nelson?
SAMMY	That's my name.
DEREK	THE Sammy Nelson.
SAMMY	I'm sure there are others.
DEREK	You're a legend, Sammy. A loyalist legend. They say you killed more Catholics during the Troubles than anyone else.
SAMMY	What makes a 'legend' in the Six Counties, eh?
DEREK	There's a big mural of you on a wall in East

	Belfast. You look younger in the mural.
SAMMY	Paintings like legends can be deceptive, Derek.
DEREK	Jesus! I don't believe it. I'm in the same jail as THE Sammy Nelson!
SAMMY	What are you in for, Derek?
DEREK	They say I threw a petrol bomb into some Paki's house.
SAMMY	Did you?
DEREK	Me and others. But they can't prove it was me ….who….
	PAUSE.
SAMMY	I take it the 'Paki' died?
DEREK	So they say….but ….
SAMMY	Couldn't you find a Catholic to attack?
DEREK	You would've. You would've. I can't believe it. Sammy Nelson.
	THE Sammy Nelson
	SAMMY GRABS DEREK BY THE THROAT.
DEREK	What are you doing, Mister Nelson?
	SAMMY RELEASES DEREK AND THROWS HIM TO GROUND.
DEREK	What was that about?
SAMMY	Fuck up, Derek.
DEREK	Sammy…..?

SAMMY	Now, listen to me, young Derek.
DEREK	I don't understand. What'd I do?
SAMMY	Of course you don't understand…..you thick stupid little gobshite.
DEREK	Hang on, Mister Nelson…….
SAMMY	Shut it, Derek. Shut it.
	DEREK COWERS IN CORNER.
SAMMY	What year were you born, Derek?
DEREK	Eh?
SAMMY	What year were you born? Do you know?
DEREK	1996.
SAMMY	1996?
DEREK	12TH of July.
	SAMMY LAUGHS.
SAMMY	12th of July. And I bet you're real proud of that. Being born on the 12TH of July.
DEREK	Yeh…..I am….
SAMMY	You were born one year before the Good Friday Agreement.
DEREK	My Da says that was a sell-out to the Taigs.
SAMMY	He does, does he?
DEREK	It was. Wasn't it?
SAMMY	You have never known the Troubles, Derek?
DEREK	Not like you, Sammy. My Da told me how it used

	to be.
SAMMY	How it used to be? TIOCFADH AR LA…..Do you
	know what that means,
	Derek?
DEREK	Taig language>
SAMMY	It means 'our day will come'. It's Gaelic. The Taigs
	as you call them, say It. Well, let me tell you
	something, young Derek, born on the 12th of July.
	OUR day is over! We Sweeneys who used to rule
	the roost. A Protestant Parliament for a
	Protestant People! We had the jobs, the shipyard,
	the Aircraft factory, the 'B' Specials, the RUC. We
	ran the place, Derek. Your Da probably told you
	that too.
DEREK	Those were the days. And Big Brexit Arlene is
	bringing them back.
SAMMY	But now your Da has no job. You have no job. All
	you have is a flag that you think you love but
	don't know why and you hate anybody who isn't a
	loyalist like you. You hate Taigs. You hate Poles.
DEREK	Poles are Taigs. I know that.
SAMMY	You hate 'Pakis' And that hatred has put you in
	jail. But that's not so bad because you think
	you've met a loyalist legend. Let me tell you about

the loyalist legend. I did do all those things during the Troubles. I killed more Catholics than anyone else. I was imprisoned. I was released. I was free to walk the streets of red white and blue Belfast again. But the colours had faded, Derek. I am back. In here. In jail. You want to know why and how? I will tell you, young Derek of 1996. I will tell you. You need to know.

DEREK   Go ahead, Sammy. I'm listening…………..

HOLD/LIGHT CHANGE

SCENE 15

ENTER DOMINIC.

DOMINIC   This......this is where the English made me into an 'activist'. An unlikely setting it would seem but a well-worn one in the history of activism. This particular well-worn dingy, scruffy, paint-peeling fried egg smelling setting is a student hostel in Cheetham Hill, in the city of Manchester. Lancashire, England. I came here to get away from the devotional novena-ed mother and her 'eternal' recitations about obeying the 'laws of God' and to do the teacher training thing. Another well-worn path that ends in 'activism'. There were more than a few teachers amongst those who fought in 1916. Pearse. Thomas Clarke. Not that I was thinking about those things in those days. More about Piaget and what good crack were the lads from the North of England. Tom, from Sunderland. Mick, from Leeds. Bright. Sharp. Irreverent. Working class. With a healthy suspicion and disdain for all societal systems especially the University one. But all that was to change....change utterly....one Sunday afternoon.

The news came through on the nineteen inch black and white Television set that the Paras had shot dead thirteen people in Derry. In what was to become known as Bloody Sunday! I can see and feel the huddle of young men staring at that television screen....in shock....in awe...in disbelief.....in the slow trickle of impotent rage that began to possess us and run down our long-haired necks. This was the end. This was the beginning. Marches. Civil Rights. Burntollet. Internment. Interrogation. Torture. And now English Prime Minister Ted Heath was ordering the Paras to 'quell the natives'....not with CS gas and rubber bullets......but with live ammunition that left bleeding bodies lying on the streets of their own city of Derry. A priest, a man of the Catholic cloth, hunched down, waving a white hankie, giving the Last Rites to those who had been butchered. This was no longer about John Hume inspired Martin Luther Kinged peaceful 'I have a dream' protests....this was a WAR! And in a war....you get killed....or kill.

That Sunday night in the student hostel in Cheetham Hill in Manchester City, Lancashire,

England I said farewell to Tom and Mick and Piaget. I took the boat home....back to Belfast....back to Northern Ireland...back to.................

SOUND OF STEADY BEAT OF BODHRAN DRUM LIGHT CHANGE.

DOMINIC   I killed three men. Three men from the Royal Ulster Constabulary. I aided and abetted in the murder of others. But those three RUC men, I did. Me. I assassinated them. I was a volunteer in the IRA. And we were at war. I was a soldier of the Irish Republican Army and I had orders. I carried out those orders. Willingly. I shot them. Dead. The operation was a success. Three dead RUC men was a coup. We had hit back at the enemy. That was three less coppers to do the things that coppers did. I was 'happy'. Yeh, happy. Happy at a job well done. There were no complications No fuckups. The job was cleanly done. The getaway was stage managed efficiently. There were no problems. No one involved got picked up for the murders. It was a success. Another blow had been struck for Ireland. For freedom. For the Republic. For the oppressed working class of Belfast. We were on the road to a full Republic. Thirty two

Counties. Free and airy. I had played my part. I

was a volunteer. I was part of a long tradition

Fenian freedom fighters. And I was, as I say,

'happy'. I watched the funerals of the three RUC

men on television with cold satisfaction. I

watched the Union Jack draped coffins. The RUC

pall bearers. I heard the Protestant Minister's

words of condemnation of the perpetrators of the

'heinous crime'. I stared through the TV screen at

the weeping, grieving widows and children of the

three RUC men and I felt nothing. No, not

nothing. I felt avenged. I felt justified. I felt as I

imagined a RUC man or a British soldier would

feel, watching the funeral of a tricolour draped

coffin. I had come a long way. A long way from

the seventeen year old who had stood in the

grounds of the Redemptorist Retreat House after

listening to the hell fire and damnation sermon of

Father Finlay. I.........had become what you call ' a

terrorist'...............

SILENCE.

DOMINIC PUTS ON BALACLAVA. PICKS UP RIFLE.

POINTS IT AT AUDIENCE.

LIGHT CHANGE.

SCENE 16

BISHOP AND FATHER ADAMS.

SILENCE.

BISHOP   I have received a letter from Rome. From the Vatican. It concerns you, Father Adams.

SILENCE.

It seems, His Holiness, Pope Francis, is going to be less tolerant than his predecessor on certain matters. You know what those certain matters are, Father Adams?

FR ADAMS   I have an idea, Your Worship.

BISHOP   The Church, as you know, has been through a very difficult period. World Wide. And here in Ireland. Changes are to be made. Radical changes, Father Adams. How long have you been a priest?

FR ADAMS   It will be twenty years in March of this year. I was ordained on my birthday.

BISHOP   And you have always served in Ireland?

FR ADAMS   Yes. I spent a year in Rome. But Ireland has been

	where I have been.
BISHOP	There have been many changes in Ireland in those years.
FR ADAMS	Many. Yes.
BISHOP	The Church has changed. The Church has declined in its power and influence. And one of the reasons for that change and decline you know about, Father Adams.
FR ADAMS	I do.
BISHOP	Repentance is one thing. Reparation is quite another.
FR ADAMS	It is, Your Worship.
BISHOP	And the Church…..Pope Francis…..is ensuring that proper reparations are made. Things that happened in the past…..things in the past that were 'overlooked' are no longer to remain in the darkness.
FR ADAMS	I understand, Your Worship.
BISHOP	Do you, 'understand'?
FR ADAMS	I do.
	SILENCE.
BISHOP	This letter, Father Adams, from the Vatican, has instructions within it that concern your future.
FR ADAMS	I have a future?

BISHOP	We all have a future until the day we are called by the Almighty.
FR ADAMS	I meant......
BISHOP	I know what you meant.
	SILENCE.
	You are to be sent to South America. To Buenos Aires, as it happens. The Lord does work in mysterious ways. Once there, you will be informed by the Bishop there, of what work you will be doing. He knows nothing of what has happened or why you are being sent to him. Whether you decide to tell him will be a matter for your own conscience.
	SILENCE.
BISHOP	That will be all, Father Adams. You may go.
	FR ADAMS MAKES TO LEAVE/EXIT.
BISHOP	Father Adams?
	FR ADAMS STOPS. TURNS TO BISHOP.
	Repentance is one thing. Reparation is another.
	THEY HOLD A LOOK.
	May God have mercy on all of us.
	HOLD. AS FR ADAMS EXITS, MRS FITZPATRICK ENTERS.
MRS F	I take it we won't be seeing Father Adams again?

SILENCE.

Of course this kind of thing would never happen if there were married priests. And women priests!

SHE PICKS UP THE WHISKEY GLASSES.

I take it these are for washing.

SHE GOES TO EXIT.

Don't forget, you have an appointment with the Minster of Education at 4pm. She's another one. Used to be a terrorist. It's all a far cry from when I was a girl and attending school with the Sisters of Mercy. Maybe I should have entered the Poor Clares and prayed for ye all.

BISHOP	That'll be all, Mrs Fitzpatrick. Thank you.
MRS F	Women priests is the only answer.

4pm.....remember, Your Worship.

EXIT MRS FITZPATRICK.

LIGHT CHANGE/SOUND OF CHOIR SINGING 'FAITH OF OUR FATHERS'.

SCENE 17

DUBLIN. POLICE STATION. INTERVIEW ROOM.

BARRY, THE DETECTIVE AND OFFICER.

DETECTIVE   Name?

BARRY   His or mine?

DETECTIVE   Your name, please.

BARRY   Barry Short.

DETECTIVE   Address?

BARRY   I don't have one. You could write down Dublin

                City. Ireland.

DETECTIVE   Occupation?

BARRY   Terrorist.

DETECTIVE   You are originally from Cork, Mister Short?

BARRY   Is that a problem for you, Detective? Jackeens

                hate Corkies, don't they?

                I can return the compliment.

DETECTIVE   Mister Short......

BARRY   You can call me Barry. Barry is my name.

DETECTIVE   Barry. Where were you between the hours of.....

BARRY   Between the hour of birth and now?

                O'HARE STEPS FORWARD. BARRY STARES AT HIM.

                LOOKS TO DETECTIVE.

BARRY   Look Detective, I'll make it easy for you. It was me. I stabbed the black fella in the Green.

DETECTIVE	You admit it?
BARRY	I do.
DETECTIVE	What weapon did you use?
BARRY	A knife. It wasn't a feckin knitting needle.
DETECTIVE	And if it was you who committed the crime, what was your motive?
BARRY	I hate Black people.
DETECTIVE	Why do you hate Black people, Barry?
BARRY	You can't explain hate, Detective. It's not susceptible to reason. Can you explain why Jackeens hate Corkies?

DETECTIVE AND O'HARE EXCHANGE ALMOST HELPLESS LOOK.

DETECTIVE	Do you know the black man you claim to have stabbed?
BARRY	I told you. It was me. I stabbed him.
DETECTIVE	'He' is a Catholic priest.
BARRY	So? What difference does that make? He's still Black. I didn't stab him because he's a priest. I didn't know he was a priest. I stabbed him cos he's feckin black?
DETECTIVE	Have you stabbed other black people?
BARRY	No. This is my first.

O'HARE	And last….
BARRY	We'll see about that.
	SILENCE.
	So, aren't you going to charge me, Detective?
	DETECTIVE AND O'HARE EXCHANGE LOOKS. AND NOD TO EXIT.
DETECTIVE	Stay here, Barry.
BARRY	Now where would I be going to, Detective? I can't walk through walls….
	yet…..
	EXIT DETECTIVE AND O'HARE.
	LIGHT CHANGE.

SCENE 18

A CEMETERY.

HARRY AND SEAN AS BEFORE.

HARRY	Would you ever think of coming back? Coming home.
SEAN	There are those who say you can never go back.
HARRY	What do you say?
SEAN	I....I.... think that I agree with them.
HARRY	Why?
SEAN	I'm not sure.
HARRY	Not sure?
SEAN	I remember years ago...in the early years after I'd left...my father said to me one time....'You'd only be content somewhere in the middle of the Irish Sea equidistant from both coastlines'. I think he might have had a point.
HARRY	So you have no home? Is that what you're saying? No roots?
SEAN	Do you?
HARRY	I do. I belong here. In Belfast. In Ireland. I am 'Irish'.
SEAN	Are you suggesting I'm not?
HARRY	You're a visitor now. A tourist.

SEAN (SMILES)	I stay in a hotel when I'm here.
HARRY	Hotels are for visitors. Tourists.
SEAN	They never forgive you for voluntary exile, do they?
HARRY	Who?
SEAN	The Irish.
HARRY	Why should they? You left them. Does a wife or husband ever forgive the spouse who left them?
SEAN	Love dies. Sometimes.
HARRY	And you have to live with the consequences.
SEAN	I do. Are there consequences for staying?
HARRY	What do you mean?
SEAN	You 'know' what I mean.
	SILENCE.
SEAN	Do you remember that time you came over to London?
HARRY	I was never in London.
SEAN	You were. You came over with a woman.
HARRY	A woman? In London?
SEAN	You were thinking of leaving Belfast.
HARRY	Me? Leaving Belfast? Nah, you've got that wrong.
SEAN	You stayed with Lucy and I in the bedsit in Paddington for about a week.
HARRY	I think you're confusing me with somebody else.

SEAN	You complained about having spuds three days in a row for the dinner.
HARRY	I've never liked spuds, it's true.
SEAN	You and the woman went looking for accommodation. I think she was pregnant.
HARRY	I have no memory of any of that.
SEAN	You came back one night and do you know what you said?
HARRY	I have no memory of any of this. You're definitely thinking of somebody else.
SEAN	It was you, alright. You, Harry.
HARRY	And what did I say?
SEAN	You 'said' that in one of the places you went to view, a black man answered the door and all you could see was his eyes and the teeth. White teeth in a black face. And you and the pregnant woman were frightened.
HARRY	Are you calling me a racist?
SEAN	That's what you said.
HARRY	I have no idea what you're talking about. I was never in London with a pregnant woman looking for a place to live.
SEAN	How long did you say you've been sick for?
HARRY	Nearly twenty years.

SEAN	This happened before that. You were fit and healthy then.
HARRY	I don't remember.
SEAN	Don't you?
	SILENCE.
	LIGHT CHANGE.

SCENE 19

	CONVENT CHAPEL. SACRED MUSIC.
	ENTER MOTHER PATRICIA FOLLOWED BY OTHER NUNS/CAST MEMBERS.
	ENTER THERESA AND JOSEPH.
	PAUSE.
	ENTER MARY MAHON, NOW WEARING A NUN'S HABIT.
	SHE WALKS SLOWLY UPSTAGE TOWARDS MOTHER PATRICIA WHO IS STANDING IN FRONT OF THE ALTAR.
	SILENCE.
MOTHER P (TO MARY)	Sister Maria Seraphina, of Our Heavenly Father.
MARY/SISTER MARIA	Lord, you have called by my new name. Behold, I come to do your holy will.
MOTHER P	Dear daughter, what do you desire?

SISTER MARIA	One thing I have asked of the Lord, this I seek, to dwell in the house of the Lord, all the days of my life.
MOTHER P	Have you pondered well and really understand what you wish to commit yourself to do?
SISTER MARIA	I have, with the grace of God.
MOTHER P	Have you the courage to trust in God completely, that He will provide for all your needs, especially that He will give you the grace to live out faithfully what you desire to promise to Him?
SISTER MARIA	I have, with the grace of God.
MOTHER P	You have put your hand to the plough and from this day forward there can be no looking back. Foxes have holes and the birds of the air have nests but the Son of Man, your Spouse, had nowhere to lay His head. Are you prepared to follow Him completely until the end?
SISTER MARIA	I am, with the grace of God.
MOTHER P	What you hold now, may you hold forever. What you promise now, may you never abandon, but with swift pace, light step and unswerving feet go forward, securely, joyfully, swiftly and prudently on the path of happiness, so that you may offer your vows---chastity, poverty,

obedience---to the Most High in that perfection to which the Spirit of the Lord has called you.

SILENCE

MOTHER PATRICIA LOWERS HER HEAD TO SISTER MARIA.

SISTER MARIA PROSTRATES HERSELF IN FRONT OF THE ALTAR.

PAUSE.

SUDDENLY THERESA LETS OUT A PRIMAL SCREAM. RUNS TOWARDS HER DAUGHTER LYING IN FRONT OF THE ALTAR, SCREAMING.

THERESA   NO! NO!

THERESA PULLS AT THE FEET OF SISTER MARIA.

BLACKOUT.

SCENE 20

DEREK AND SAMMY. IN JAIL.

SILENCE

SAMMY   You see, Derek when I got out after fifteen years inside, I realised the rage was still in me. I couldn't settle. In fact I was more unhappy and fucked up upon my release than when I was in jail. In jail I knew where I was. Literally and mentally. There was a pattern to life….a structure. I had friends. Friends who were experiencing the same as me. We 'knew' each other. Aye, there were some mouthy gobshites……there always is but there fewer of them in jail than in the outside world. And then there was the wife. The wife! We were married when she was eighteen. I was twenty. We had four years of marriage before I was imprisoned. At the beginning, the early years of my incarceration, she visited like all the others. 'I'll love you forever. I'll be here when you get out. No other man will ever be to me what you are'. It's amazing, Derek, what women can say to a man when he's down and the man believes it. But life, Derek, women and men are not like that. There are no angels. There is no such thing as faithfulness….'love forever'. And what happened, happened. I'd heard rumours. Chitty chat about her supposed antics when I was still inside. The visits from her stopped. I heard more stories…true or not I didn't know. Did it matter? Stories are stories. But when I got out what I found wasn't nice, Derek. Wasn't nice at all. My one time wife, the beautiful eighteen year old I had married was old. Old like myself. Ugly. Like I had got ugly. Ugly inside. She was a reflection of me and what I had become in the intervening years. And she was a drunk like I might have been if I'd had access to it in jail. And she was whoring her way round Belfast and most of the six counties by all accounts. She was a drunken, blowsy harlot with a throwback head laugh for any Tom Dick or Harry that would ply her with drink before he fucked her to hell and back.

SAMMY APPEARS TO NEARLY BREAK DOWN IN TEARS.

DEREK   Sammy….Sammy? Please. Don't cry. Sammy

Nelson never cries. You're a legend.

SAMMY GRABS DEREK BY THE THROAT.

SAMMY
So you know what I did, Derek........you know what I did....I slit her throat from ear to ear.........

SAMMY MAKES THROAT CUTTING GESTURE ACROSS DEREK WHO IS NOW VERY FRIGHTENED.

......and as the blood poured from her neck and her eyes bulged in her head looking at me.....looking at me.....with.......'love'....I smeared her blood all over my face....and hers....so that we both looked like characters from a cheap horror film.........the horror! The horror!

SAMMY RELEASES DEREK AND TOSSES HIM ASIDE.

SILENCE.

DEREK
You are still a legend to me....Sammy Nelson....Sammy Nelson.....

SAMMY BEGINS TO KICK AND BEAT DEREK IN A FRENZY.

LIGHT CHANGE/ SOUND OF LOUD SCREAM/ DEREK/WOMAN/SAMMY.

SCENE 21

ENTER DOMINIC.

DOMINIC

I still believe that violence is the only way to change things. For let's face it, the Peace Process such as it is, would not be happening if there hadn't been the campaign of violence. The Brits would not have come to the negotiating table if we hadn't hit them with the city of London bombs. The golden mile in London town wants to do business. Implement capitalism. And it's hard to do if all the windows of the Lloyds Building are blown out and the desk computers with share prices on screen aren't flickering brightly and the Banks of the World are thinking Frankfurt is safer! And then there's our 'separated brethren'. The Protestants. The Unionists. The loyalists. Nothing's going to get the Sweeney Todds to share the bag of sweets unless the Brits and Yanks squeeze their balls a bit and even then they'll still resist. 'We are not surrendering that bag of sweets. That yellow man and honeycomb you used to get from the shop in Sandy Row is OURS! Ulster is Right! Ulster will Fight! But against all that politics', as my mother would have said, what's really changed? The waves still lap and sometimes crash against the Antrim coast. People still get up in the morning to go to work if they have work to go to. They fall in and out of love. They row with each other over whose copy of the Irish News, Newsletter or Belfast Telegraph is telling the truth. They still enjoy a big Ulster fry with dipped bread. They still banter and sleg each other in that distinctive Belfast Northern way. They still hate the South. It all still goes on. Except for those in the cemeteries. Some of those who went before their natural time. The Hunger Strikers. The three RUC I murdered. Nothing's changed. And everything's changed. I think I have changed. I am older. I am disillusioned. It is common with one time activists. I am sadder. But what sorrow has produced the sadness? I am not sure. I am not sure I know the answer to that one. I am not sure I feel sorry for killing the three RUC men. And yet I do have this feeling I should repent. I did break the Fifth Commandment.

THOU SHALT NOT KILL! I do feel I should make reparation. Recompense for that 'sin'. And yet when I think back to those times I can still recognise feeling 'happy'. I got away with it. Maybe that's it. Maybe at the time I felt it was a crime. A sin. I would be punished for it. I'd do time in jail. I'd be killed by one of them. I wasn't.

I didn't do time for that particular action. It is bugging me. It is more than bugging me. It is a piece of unfinished business in my life that I need to do something about. I am thinking of giving myself up. Handing myself in. Going to the police station and asking them to arrest me, charge me, punish me. It's not because I remember Father Finlay's sermon. About hell. Burning. Eternity. It is because I feel and think it would be the RIGHT thing to do.

LIGHT CHANGE/MUSIC

DOMINIC   They weren't interested. The Northern Ireland Police Authority didn't want to know. At first, they thought I was mad. Another headcase with a crazy story of what they'd done 'in the troubles'. They said it wasn't uncommon for fellas to go in and tell them all about the crimes they had committed. The said there was a whole load of people in Northern Ireland, in the Six Counties, felt they'd been left out if they hadn't been involved in the action. They said there were some people in the Six Counties suffering from Post Troubles trauma. And that I was probably one of those. They said I probably missed the security gates in town, the bomb scares in Marks and Spencer of a Saturday afternoon, being stopped and searched by the Army. They said, I probably missed the noise of riots, bin lids being battered, gunfire and sirens. They said, there was a whole load of people couldn't stand the peace. The normality. The banality of everyday existence. They said there were people who had stopped watching or listening to the news because WE, Northern Ireland, was not on it in the same way as in the olden days. They told me to go about my business and not to bother them anymore. I'd get over it eventually. I'd get used to the banality of normal life in time. But I shot dead three of you fellas. Doesn't that mean anything to you? There were a lot of us shot dead, they said. And we shot dead some of you people. But they are dead and gone, they said. And you ranting and raving about how you were responsible isn't going to bring them back. But what about 'justice' I said? At that point they all laughed. And called out to each other. There's a fella in here talking about 'justice'. The laughter grew more raucous and loud. Besides, one of them said, the Government introduced an amnesty. Even if what you say is true and you did kill three RUC men in the seventies, nobody's going to do anything about it. It is gone, my friend, they said. It is the past. And the past is a foreign country. Historians will write about it, they said, and we both know they'll get it wrong. Only those who were there then KNOW. And with death, that KNOWING will disappear altogether. It will be in the box with the worms. And the worms will eat away at it until there is nothing left. Nothing. Nothing!

What now Dominic? Am I to live with it? Am I never to receive Absolution? Should I track down the three RUC widows and ask for.....for what? Is it best left with the worms?

SILENCE.

This.....this....is Milltown Cemetery. Falls Road.

Belfast. Northern Ireland. This is where they lay
you to rest.......bury you.....if you were killed in
action by British Forces......died on hunger
strike.....this is where they make you into
a.....what?.....martyr?.....a dead fighter for the
freedom of Ireland....Ireland unfree shall never be
at peace....Too long a sacrifice can make a stone
of the heart.....Did that play of mine send out men
the English shot?

I was here last Christmas Eve....in Milltown
cemetery....it was cold......Colder than death
itself......six inches of snow lay on the
ground.....not a soul was to be seen or heard....it
was.....it was.....BEAUTIFUL.....haunting.....the
headstones, crosses, memorial plaques
looked.......strangely defiant........even the crooked
ones, the sagging ones, the ones fallen in on
themselves.....their cloaks of snow made them like
mute angels....the sun's rays fell across them like a
conductor's baton.....urging them to sing.....join in
the chorus.....the chorus of souls.....like
snowflakes falling ....falling all over the
cemetery.....Milltown cemetery....all over the Falls
Road....all over Belfast City.....all over 'Northern'

Ireland........

Crucified Jesus! Have Mercy Upon Us!

LIGHT CHANGE/SILENCE/HOLD.

SCENE 22

BISHOP AND JACINTA REID, MINISTER FOR
EDUCATION AT STORMONT.

BISHOP	You've come a long way. Miss Reid….
JACINTA	Not really. I live up the road from here.
BISHOP	I didn't mean today, Miss….how should I address you? Minister? Miss Reid?
JACINTA	Jacinta is my name.
BISHOP	Jacinta? One of the three children of Fatima.
JACINTA	My mother had a special devotion to Our Lady of Fatima.
BISHOP	A wise and devout woman your mother. Is she……
JACINTA	No. She died in 1986.
BISHOP	May her soul rest in peace. No doubt, she would be happy, if she were alive, at how far we have all come. And you, now, being in the Government.
JACINTA	My mother had no interest in politics. I get that from my father.
BISHOP	And is he?

JACINTA	Dead. Five years after my mother.
BISHOP	Sad. I am sure he would be proud of you and your current position. It's a long way from being in Armagh jail back in those terrible times.
JACINTA	Those 'terrible times' were not of our making.
BISHOP	Not entirely. We have the English to blame for some of it. But Mister Blair did see the light and did help to put us on the road to peace.
	JACINTA SHRUGS. SAYS NOTHING.
BISHOP	And he has become a Catholic.
	AGAIN JACINTA SAYS NOTHING.
BISHOP	Please, Jacinta. Do take a seat. She is a saint now.
JACINTA	Who?
BISHOP	Jacinta of Fatima.
JACINTA	I am not a saint.
BISHOP	Few are, Miss Reid. Few are. I have asked to see you to seek clarification on a few rumours that have been doing the rounds. I am sure there is nothing in them but I thought we could clear the air. And I could make known to you the position of the Catholic Church.
JACINTA	I am all for 'clearing the air', Your Worship.
BISHOP	Catholic education. Catholic schools are a very important part of being a Catholic. I don't need to

	tell you that. I'm sure you benefited from such an education yourself.
JACINTA	Some of the nuns who taught me might not think so.
BISHOP	You went to the nuns? Convent educated?
JACINTA	Saint Dominic's.
BISHOP	A very fine school. Always was and will continue to be so. It is unfortunate that there are not so many nuns teaching there as once was. But sadly, vocations are not what they once were. Fewer young women these days are devoting themselves to the service of God.
	Did you ever consider it, Jacinta?
JACINTA	I prayed for a vocation from the age of eight until twelve, Your Worship. But that call never came. Other things intervened.
BISHOP	Indeed. 'Other things'. My concern, Jacinta, is that there has been some talk of abolishing denominational schools. Or at least, in these hard economic times, amalgamating Catholic and State/Protestant schools. And while we, the Catholic Church, have no problem cooperating and working together with others, we would not want to see our Catholic way of life being

	undermined. We have enough problems with the secular world in which we live these days..
JACINTA	Your Worship. I understand your concerns. But I have not heard of any such moves.
BISHOP	And as Minister of Education you would know if there were such moves?
JACINTA	There are none.
BISHOP	But these rumours are disturbing.
JACINTA	Rumours are always disturbing, Your Worship. But rumours are rumours and I can assure you there is no substance to any of them.
BISHOP	I have your assurance on that, Minister?
JACINTA	You do. That said…..
BISHOP	Yes…..
JACINTA	I have no control over what people talk about. The people are free to discuss such issues. Freedom of debate is one of the things that I hope we have attained in our more open society. All of our old ways of thinking are up for examination if we are to move forward and create a better society for the people of Northern Ireland.
BISHOP	An admirable ambition, Minister. One the Catholic Church fully supports.
JACINTA	That is encouraging, Your Worship.

BISHOP	I hope you understand, Minister, that the Catholic Church cannot move on some matters. Not out of intransigence or indeed Church interests as is sometimes suggested by some, but because there are some matters that belong to God.
JACINTA	And some to Caesar. Perhaps, we understand each other more than we think.
BISHOP	I do hope so….Jacinta.
JACINTA	Hope has made me the Minister of Education, Your Worship.
BISHOP	Yes…..well, if you'll excuse me, I do have another appointment as I'm sure you do too. People like us measure our lives out in meetings and appointments.
JACINTA	Yes. We do. I am scheduled to attend a concert at one of our 'State' Schools.
BISHOP	I hope they play music to your taste.
JACINTA	I have a very catholic taste in music, Your Worship.
	ENTER MRS FITZPATRICK. EXIT JACINTA.
MRS FITZ	Well?
BISHOP	She learnt more in Armagh Prison than she did in St Dominic's, that one.
MRS FITZ	Didn't I tell you? Didn't I tell you?

BISHOP	Pour me a small one, please. And pour one for yourself.
	MRS FITZPATRICK POURS THE WHISKEY. SHE AND THE BISHOP CLINK GLASSES.
MRS FITZ	She'd need to get up a lot earlier in the morning to fool you, Your Worship.
BISHOP	I am not sure she 'sleeps' at all, Ms Fitzpatrick.
	THE BISHOP LOOKS TOWARDS WHERE JACINTA
EXITED.	
	LIGHT CHANGE.

SCENE 23

	DUBLIN. HOSPITAL WARD.
	FR FLANNAGAN, MAGEE AND O'HARE.
MAGEE	We have arrested a young man who admits to stabbing you, Father Flannagan.
FR FLANNAGAN	Do you believe him? Do you think it was he who did it?
	MAGEE AND O'HARE EXCAHNGE LOOKS.
MAGEE	I don't know. He's a strange one. He confessed to it immediately.
O'HARE	He's a cocky wee fecker.

MAGEE	He's not stupid. In fact.....
O'HARE	He was very blatant about why he did it.
FR FLANNAGAN	Which was?
O'HARE	He said it was because you are......black......
FR FLANNAGAN	I am not the first, Sgt. O'Hare.
O'HARE	No. I suppose not.
MAGEE	I told him you were a priest.
O'HARE	He said, what difference does that make? He's black.
FR FLANNAGAN	On that, he is right.
MAGEE	Would you be able to identify him, Father Flannagan?
FR FLANNAGAN	Without question. He passed by me a couple of times before he......in fact, we exchanged looks. I spoke to him.
O'HARE	You spoke to him?
FR FLANNAGAN	Yes. He was standing behind the bench. I turned to ask if I could help. He ran off. Then when he came back.....well, you know what happened then.
O'HARE	That clinches it. We have positive identification.
MAGEE	We'll see.
O'HARE	What do you mean we'll see. It's cut and dry, Pat. The Father says he saw him. Spoke to him. That's

	good enough for me and for any court in the land even a Dublin one.
MAGEE	I suppose you're right.
FR FLANNAGAN	You don't seem convinced, Detective Magee? I can assure you my eyesight is good. I did see who stabbed me.
MAGEE	I don't doubt you, Father Flannagan.
FR FLANNAGAN	You just don't understand why he did it?
O'HARE	Hate is not susceptible to reason. He said that.
FR FLANNAGAN	He is right about that too. Like you said, Detective, he is not stupid.
MAGEE	No. Not stupid.
FR FLANNAGAN	I have a favour to ask of you, Detective. And I know my request will seem odd and not part of your usual procedure.
MAGEE	What is it?
FR FLANNAGAN	Would you bring the young man to see me?
O'HARE	What? Here? In the hospital?
MAGEE	If you wish.
O'HARE	Pat?
MAGEE	Shut up, O'Hare.
O'HARE	Pat……
MAGEE	I'll do as you ask, Father Flannagan.
FR FLANNAGAN	Thank you.

MAGEE INDICATES TO O'HARE TO LEAVE. AS HE
DOES, NURSE BURNS ENTERS.

O'HARE   Eileen, how are you? Jasus, you're looking grand.
                Uniform suits you.

THEY EXIT. FR FLANNAGAN SMILES.

MAGEE   I wouldn't encourage him. He's a married man
                with four kids.

FR FLANNAGAN   Lust doesn't obey reason either, Detective.

PAUSE.

MAGEE   I'll bring the young man along to see you. Though
                what you're going to say him or what good it'll do,
                I have no idea.

FR FLANNAGAN   What is his name?

MAGEE   Barry. Barry Short. He's from Cork. You might
                have some difficulty understanding his accent.

FR FLANNAGAN   I understand you and the Sgt.

MAGEE   Forgive me, Father Flannagan. Can I ask you a
                question before I leave.

FR FLANNAGAN   What is it?

MAGEE   How did someone like you end up with a name
                like Patrick Flannagan?

FR FLANNAGAN LAUGHS. THEN WINCES AND
PUTS HIS HAND TO HIS SIDE.

FR FLANNAGAN   It is a long story, Detective. I will tell you another time. Suffice to say, you Irish get around a bit.

MAGEE NODS. HALF-SMILES.

EXITS. LIGHT CHANGE.

SCENE 24

A CEMETERY.

HARRY AND SEAN.

HARRY	I suppose you have people belonging to you in here?
SEAN	I do. The parents. An uncle, two aunts and a cousin. And an uncle I never knew. Dead before I arrived.
HARRY	Is that all?
SEAN	There's a load of them up in Hannahstown.
HARRY	Nice spot. Hannahstown.
SEAN	There's one in Our Lady's Acre and another two in Carnmoney.
HARRY	Scattered, then.
SEAN	And you?
HARRY	They're all in here. Falls Road people go to Milltown. When the time comes I'll come here as well.

SEAN	You will?
HARRY	Definitely. Where else would I go? And you? Will they bring you 'home' to bury you?
SEAN	Who knows?
HARRY	Or will they bury you in 'English' soil….in London?
SEAN	I've lived most of my life there so I suppose……….
HARRY	Exiled in death as in life.
SEAN	Maybe….
HARRY	Have you noticed how many of those who went away clearly gave instructions to be brought back for burial?
SEAN	Who?
HARRY	Heaney's in Bellaghy not far from the farm of his childhood.
SEAN	I've visited.
HARRY	It's a peaceful little churchyard. Montague. Brought back to Tyrone after his travels away.
SEAN	Why do you think that is?
HARRY	I don't 'know'. But I imagine they feel a debt to the place of their origins. Do you?
SEAN	I'm not sure I'd use the word debt. Where you're born after all is an accident. As the man said, he was born in wherever because at the time he wanted to be near his mother.

HARRY	Bit of a wit, that man.
SEAN	Debt. Not sure. Influence. Yes.
HARRY	It gave you your material.
SEAN	Some. Not all.
HARRY	The good stuff. The real stuff.
	SEAN SHRUGS.
SEAN	Clay is the word.
	Clay is the flesh.
HARRY	Screams the apocalypse of clay
	In every corner of this land.
	LIGHT CHANGE.

SCENE 25

A SANITORIUM.

THERESA SITS ON A ROCKING CHAIR BY THE
WINDOW LOOKING OUT INTO SPACE.

SHE ROCKS BACK AND FORTH.

SHE IS DRESSED IN A NIGHTGOWN AND DRESSING
GOWN. HER HAIR IS UNKEMPT AND WILD. HER
FEET ARE BARE AND TWITCHING.

SILENCE.

ENTER A NUN WITH JOSEPH. THE NUN SILENTLY
INDICATES TO JOSEPH

TO ENTER.

JOSEPH SLOWLY, QUIETLY GOES TOWARD

THERESA. HE SITS ON A CHAIR NEARBY.

SILENCE.

JOSEPH   Theresa……..

Theresa…………..

THERESA'S ROCKING GETS FASTER AND FASTER.

SHE PAWS AT HER FACE AND HAIR.

SLOW FADE.

SPOT ON CRUCIFIX HANGING ON THE WALL.

BLACKOUT.

SCENE 26

SILENCE.

IN BLACKOUT, WE HEAR THE SLOW BEAT OF A

LAMBEG DRUM.

THE LIGHTS VERY SLOWLY FADE UP.

THE DRUM BEAT BUILDS TO A FRENZIED CLIMAX.

AT CRESCENDO/CUT

SPOT ON DEREK.

HE IS HANGING FROM A BAR UPSTAGE. AN

ORANGE SASH AROUND HIS NECK.

HOLD. BLACKOUT.

SCENE 27

ENTER DOMINIC.

DOMINIC   Before the Troubles, there were 1,000 people in

jail in Northern Ireland. When Long Kesh closed,

10,000 prisoners had passed through its gates.

I was one of those 10,000. But the Kesh is gone.

Grass grows over what had been one of the

largest internment camps ever. It is history now.

And history will be written, rewritten, revised,

used and abused. Even those of us who were in

there and witnessed 'the dirty protest', the

torture, the beatings, the hunger strikes, the slow

deaths of young men, the brutality of the

guards…..our memories will be coloured by the

passage of time. But time doesn't heal wounds.

It simply forgets. Blurs the vision, appears in

books, plays….regurgitated versions of what

happened. Fodder for professional historians and

smug arrogant careerist professors of 'Irish

Studies'. Footnotes in the long story of relations

between England and Ireland. Governments of

the day will make the past fit their versions of the present and those who were there will remain dead and silent. 'As for man his days are as grass for the wind bloweth over it and it is gone'. The wind blows over the grass of Long Kesh. Those of us still here strain to hear its whisperings.

There is a graveyard in Bellaghy, in County Derry. Northern Ireland. It has become a place of pilgrimage for in one quiet corner under an oak tree is the grave of the Northern Irish poet, Seamus Heaney. 'I shouldered a kind of manhood stepping in to lift the coffins of dead relations'. They lie near him. His dead relations. In Bellaghy cemetery. Across the lane in another section of that country churchyard lie two Irish rebels. Two of the ten men who died on Hunger Strike in 1981. Francis Hughes, after 59 days on hunger strike. Thomas McIlwee, after 62 days. Under the clay of Bellaghy, three men of Northern Ireland. Two sides of the Irish coin. The poet and the rebel. The pen and the gun. They lie silently together in the same earth. The grey stone Church in the middle of Bellaghy cemetery........broods........'maybe as cold/And passionate as the dawn'..............

LIGHT CHANGE.

SCENE 28

DUBLIN. HOSPITAL WARD.

FR FLANNAGAN IS SITTING UP IN BED. HE IS

READING ALOUD.

FR FLANNAGAN   The time will come

when with elation

you will greet yourself arriving

at your own door, in your own mirror

and each will smile at the other's welcome

and say, sit here. Eat.

You will love again the stranger who was your

self.

Give wine. Give bread. Give back your heart

to itself, to the stranger who has loved you

all your life, whom you ignored

for another, who knows you by heart.

Take down the love letters from the bookshelf,

the photographs, the desperate notes

peel your own image from the mirror.

Sit. Feast on life.

ENTER NURSE BURNS

NURSE BURNS   Don't stop on my account, Father Flannagan.
I just came to check you were comfortable before your visitor arrives. What is it you're reading? It 'sounds' good,

FR FLANNAGAN   Some poetry. By a Caribbean poet. Derek Walcott.

NURSE BURNS   I like poetry. Don't always understand it but I like it. We have Seamus Heaney. We 'had' Seamus Heaney. He died. I often think of his wife. What must it be like for her now after living all those years with a famous Poet. It must leave such a gaping big hole. He was from the North of course. One of ours. One of our own. Read to me, some of your Caribbean fella.

FR FLANNAGAN BEGINS TO READ THE SAME POEM.

ENTER DETECTIVE MAGEE.

FR FLANNAGAN	Detective Magee. Would you like to join our poetry group?
NURSE BURNS	I don't get it but it sounds 'beautiful' when you read it in 'that voice'.
FR FLANNAGAN	I will get you a volume. A little thank you present for looking after me so well.
NURSE BURNS	Don't bother, Father. It wouldn't be the same without you reading it.
	That voice!
	NURSE BURNS EXITS. BEAMING.
	SILENCE.
	FR FLANNAGAN PUTS BOOK ASIDE.
MAGEE	He's just outside. Are you sure about this, Father Flannagan?
FR FLANNAGAN	I am. Bring him in.
	MAGEE EXITS. RE-ENTERS WITH O'HARE AND BARRY.
	O'HARE LEADS BARRY TO CHAIR AT SIDE OF BED.
FR FLANNAGAN	I am pleased to meet you…again….Barry….
	FR FLANNAGAN PUTS OUT HIS HAND.
	BARRY DOESN'T MOVE OR LOOK AT FR FLANNAGAN
	MAGEE GOES TO SIT ON CHAIR ON OTHER SIDE.
FR FLANNAGAN	Perhaps, you would be kind enough to leave us

alone….for a little while…..

MAGEE AND O'HARE LOOK ANXIOUSLY AT EACH
OTHER.

FR FLANNAGAN NODS TO THEM TO LEAVE.

THEY EXIT.

SILENCE.

FR FLANNAGAN   I'll tell you something about myself. Then, maybe,
you can tell me something about yourself.
PAUSE.

FR FLANNAGAN   My name is Patrick Flannagan. I was born in a
place called Montserrat in the Caribbean.
Montserrat is sometimes known as the 'Emerald
Isle of the Pacific'.. My ancestors were African
slaves who took on the name of their masters.
A lot of…..black people….in Montserrat….have
Irish surnames. Ryan. O'Brien. Flannagan. I went
to a school which was run by nuns. Irish nuns. It
was the nuns who taught me to read and write. It
was the Irish nuns who taught me to love poetry.
Sister Mary Fitzpatrick. I could listen to her voice
for hours and hours. Then I went to a school run
by priests. Some of them were Irish. Some English.
One or two were…..black….from Montserrat.
My Spiritual Advisor was Father McNamara.

He was born in Montserrat. It was he who

asked if I ever wondered whether I might have a

vocation for the priesthood. Eventually, I decided

that maybe I did. I entered the seminary. I met

more Irish priests. When I was ordained I worked

in a parish where the biggest feast day....the

biggest festival of the year....was St Patrick's Day.

We had bunting and streamers....green white and

gold....and a large statue of St Patrick. A ceili band.

Dancing. Calypso songs as well. Then I was sent to

Rome.....to study....and now....now....here I am in

Ireland......where the Flannagans are from......the

Flannagans who were slave owners all those years

ago.................

SUDDENLY, BARRY LETS OUT AN ALMIGHTY

SCREAM. JUMPS FROM THE CHAIR AND ATTACKS

FR FLANNAGAN. HIS FISTS FLAILING IN A MAD

FRENZY.

ENTER MAGEE AND O'HARE AND NURSE BURNS.

MAGEE AND O'HARE GRAB BARRY AND SUBDUE

HIM ENOUGH FOR NURSE BURNS TO INJECT HIM

WITH A SYRINGE. BARRY SLUMPS ACROSS THE

BED.

HOLD.

LIGHT CHANGE.

SCENE 29

THE CONVENT.

SISTER MARIA & JOSEPH.

SISTER MARIA	How is she?
JOSEPH	The same. No change.
	SILENCE.
SISTER MARIA	And you?
JOSEPH	I'm fine. I keep myself busy. I have taken up playing bowls.
SISTER MARIA	Bowls?
JOSEPH	You know….on the Green….what retired people do. There are some young fellas play. But mostly it's those who are waiting to………
SISTER MARIA	Dad?
	JOSEPH SHAKES HIS HEAD.
JOSEPH	There's nothing to say, Mary. I mean, Sister Maria.
	SISTER MARIA SMILES.
	A BELL RINGS/THREE TIMES.
SISTER MARIA	That's the bell for prayers. I'll have to go.
	SHE MAKES TO GO.

JOSEPH	I'll come again next month…..if that's alright?
SISTER MARIA	I'll see you then.
	SISTER MARIA EXITS SWIFTLY.
JOSEPH	Pray for me, Mary. Pray for us.
	SOUND OF NUNS SINGING---TANTUM ERGO.
	LIGHT CHANGE.
	REPEAT PR0LOGUE SECTION OF 'MOTHER IRELAND' BUT WITH MUSIC/SINGING WINDING DOWN AS IN DAMAGED RECORD………..
	THE END.

26810319R00063

Printed in Poland
by Amazon Fulfillment
Poland Sp. z o.o., Wrocław